Blue Collar Goodbyes

Also by Sue Doro

Of Birds and Factories
Heart, Home and Hard Hats

BLUE COLLAR GOODBYES

Sue Doro

Papier-Mache Press
Watsonville, California

First Edition
ISBN: 0-918949-22-X Paperback
ISBN: 0-918949-23-8 Hardcover

Printed in the United States of America

Design by Cynthia Heier

Typography by Metro Typography

Thanks and acknowledgement to the following magazines and anthologies for original publication of works included in this collection: *Tradeswomen Magazine, Mill Hunk Herald, Talkin' Union, Forward Motion, Labor Notes, Village Voice, Crossing the Mainstream* (Silverleaf Press), *If I Had a Hammer* (Papier-Mache Press), *Overtime* (West End Press and Piece of the Hunk Press), *Labor and the Post-Industrial Age* (Pig Iron Press).

Photo credits: p. 63 Stephanie Doane; back cover Margaret Randall. All other photographs by Sue Doro.

Library of Congress Cataloging-in-Publication Data

Doro, Sue, 1937-
    Blue collar goodbyes / Sue Doro.—1st ed.
        p.   cm.
    Includes bibliographical references.
    ISBN 0-918949-23-8 (hardcover : acid free) : $12.00 —
ISBN 0-918949-22-X (paperback : acid free) : $8.00
        1. Working class—Wisconsin—Milwaukee—Poetry. 2.
Plant shutdowns—Wisconsin—Milwaukee—Poetry. 3.
Milwaukee (Wis.)—Poetry. I. Title
PS3554.0679B58 1992
811'.54—dc20
                                                    92-8310
                                                    CIP

To my friends from the former Milwaukee Road Railway and Allis Chalmers Corporation Tractor Shop, Milwaukee, Wisconsin, as well as the hundreds of thousands of other workers and their families who have been, and continue to be, subjected to the pain of plant closures and loss of livelihood through no fault of their own.

CONTENTS

FOREWORD

Sue Doro brings to *Blue Collar Goodbyes* a marvelous precision and skill with words that matches the impressive precision and skill she applied to metal in her many years as a railway machinist. Her wonderful poems and stories also resonate with a deep concern for people—the same affection and care for others that has found expression in her working life at her lathe, as an active participant in the women-in-trades movement, and currently as a fighter for equal opportunity in employment.

The focus of this new volume of work is the human cost of plant closings. Sue, speaking passionately and accurately from within the experiences she describes, depicts the events, personalities, emotions, and the forms of resistance that accompany this tragic development now widespread across North America.

With humor, wit, sensitivity, anger, and enormous literary power, Sue Doro's poems and stories unflinchingly demonstrate the full range of human reactions to economic destruction. But while her writing shows the devastating consequences of plant closings to individuals, families, and whole communities, it also masterfully presents the kernels of hope and joy found in working women's and men's responses to what has happened to them. In this way *Blue Collar Goodbyes* brings the light of illumination and love and struggle into a dark time.

TOM WAYMAN

ACKNOWLEDGEMENTS

Blue Collar Goodbyes was initially self-published in a different form, early in 1991, with the help of a group of caring friends, including talented artist Barry Chersky. Only five hundred copies were printed, and they're all out "there" somewhere, many in factories, labor union halls, and adult literacy classes. This new companion will now join the first edition, like a friendly coworker, with a life of its own.

My warmest thanks to Papier-Mache Press editor Sandra Martz for publishing *Blue Collar Goodbyes*. Sandra and her wonderful staff, Laurie Jones Neighbors and Dan Haldeman, labored lovingly to create this special second edition, complete with photographs.

The photos inside these pages are of real people living and working in the heartland of this country. Their lives created the words of the poems and stories in this book. They represent not only themselves and their unique personalities, but also the music of the working class. I was able to take most of the photos the last few days before the railroad shut down. They are a piece of history. My sincere thanks to all of the folks who allowed their pictures to be included. They are: Earl Mays, "Doc," Ray Fligge, Verona Guinn, John Becker, Lou Hultman, Don Hoag, Jesusita Garza, and Sylvester Walcheske.

My deepest appreciation also goes to all those who helped "machine" this book. They gave me the confidence I needed to make time outside of my day job for it all to happen. Thanks especially to my husband Larry Robbin for his meaningful and patient input as well as encouragement during the process of writing and birthing *Blue Collar Goodbyes*. In addition to Larry's ongoing support for my writing, I also believe I wouldn't have survived my nearly thirteen years on shop floors as the only female machinist, without Larry at home as my partner. His co-parenting of our five children in the often complicated role of stepfather was a challenge he met with love and determination. Thanks is too small a word for Larry.

Blue Collar Goodbyes happened. I didn't make it up. Names were changed in only two poems, "Red Dust" and "Picture of a Backward Worker." I hope you enjoy sharing the experiences.

THE CULTURAL WORKER

The poem waited for her outside the wheel shop door in the Menomonee Valley train yard. Waited, as if it were one of the countless raw cast-iron train wheels propped upright against the factory wall in the moonlight. Train wheels in long, neat rows leaning like round rusty-brown, 500-pound dominoes. Train wheels waiting to be machined.

So too, the poem waited. It had been waiting for her to finish work since 3:30 that afternoon. Now it was midnight. Soon she would step out of second shift into the dark of the going home night.

Hours ago in the early evening, the summer sun hung low and rosy over sidetracked freight cars in the yard. The poem had gone to look in the window nearest the machine the woman was operating that night. The poem thought that the sunset would surely get her attention. But then it saw her leaning across the table of a boring-mill machine, measuring inside the hub of a freight car wheel with her micrometer. She was straining on tiptoes to reach across the machine's table to the wheel's freshly cut center, and the poem could see she was too busy to be thinking poem words, so it did what it knew how to do.

It waited.

Measuring minutes against the sun's shadows on the dirty cream-colored brick wall, it waited. When five o'clock break time arrived, it waited and watched through a different window as the woman ate half her sandwich sitting at the lunch table by the men's locker room. She was sharing a newspaper and conversation with some of her coworkers. She kept on talking as she reached under the table to feed a bit of cheese to a dusty yellow, scrawny factory cat that grabbed the scrap of food in its mouth and bolted away.

The woman was the only female in the shop, and there were nights when she was lonely for the company of other women. But tonight the poem saw she was having a good time, laughing and joking with her work "buddies."

It was an hour and a half later when the poem checked in again. The woman was standing at the same machine working on a different wheel, listening intently to a short leathery-faced man with a chin full of gray quarter-inch whiskers. He wore a work-scratched green hard hat low over his dark eyes. His hands hung at his sides, glistening with soiled brown train bearing grease. In one hand he held a red-handled putty knife used to scrape lard-like gobs of grease off old train bearings. In his other hand, by their cuffs, he grasped a pair of oily black rubber gloves. The ring finger was missing on that hand. A cigarette bobbed up and down in his lips as he spoke, its ashes dusting the man's brown shirt every so often. The poem moved in closer to hear the conversation above the roar and clatter of the machine. It could catch only a few of the man's mumbling phrases: "love her . . . the kids don't talk . . . need more time." The woman was concentrating on the man's hesitant sentences with one eye on the boring-mill's cutting tool, ready to slap the stop button and flip the lever that pulled the cutting bar out of the wheel's center.

The poem went back to wait at the door until dinner break.

In summer, it was still light at eight o'clock in the evening when the break whistle blew, and the poem knew that the woman would go outside to relax on the long bench against the building. Most of the other second shifters would travel up the hill to the tavern, so she was generally alone. Some evenings after eating the rest of her saved sandwich, she'd take a stroll along the railroad tracks heading under the nearby freeway.

The walk was quiet and calming except for the faint rumble of cars far overhead. And if she walked a little further,

2

the traffic noise faded completely. There was a small stream at that end of the valley, and a hill where she'd sit and gaze at the water, listening to it ripple over rocks and chunks of cement. Wildflowers grew along the riverbanks. In springtime there were baby asparagus plants and tiny green onions hidden in the tall, waving grass. Once when she brought a spray of yellow daisies back to the shop, one of the guys found and washed a mayonnaise jar to use as a vase. The flowers lit up the tool bench by the window, and everyone that passed by that night stopped to smell the daisies or to comment on the display. She was pleasantly surprised and happy that not one man teased her about it.

Other evenings found the woman writing in her journal. But tonight there was neither a walk nor journal writing happening at dinner break, and she wasn't alone. When the poem came around the corner of the building, it saw her leaning forward on the bench, holding a small open book and flipping through its pages. She referred to certain passages by tapping the index finger of her right hand on the page while she and a group of seven or eight men seemed to be talking at the same time: "contract ... bargaining ... Chicago ... layoffs in July ... four guys fired ... bankruptcy ... they can't ... it's illegal ... they'll try." The poem decided it was fruitless to try to get into her head. Then the sound of a factory whistle pierced the air, and moments later a foreman appeared in the doorway motioning everyone back to work.

The sun was beginning to slide down behind the freeway overpass. The poem stayed outside.

At ten o'clock the poem looked in the window by the woman again. She was staring out into the deep blackness of the night without even noticing the poem. Her eyes were taking in moonlight silhouettes of axles, train wheels, and oil drums. She watched three crows gliding like slow motion, velvet shadows in front of a glowing pink yard light—one of the many fifty-foot-tall globes illuminating the train yard. A shop cat scampered over a discarded train bearing lying in the grass at the base of the pole. A warm west wind brushed the woman's cheek. She sniffed the air, smiling a little, and the poem thought for a moment that she was thinking poem thoughts. She wasn't. She was simply relieved that the night smelled of sweet Menomonee Valley city wilderness thanks to the west wind, instead of the stockyards to the east of the wheel shop.

"A few more wheels," she commented aloud to no one in particular, and then turned away from the window. Thoughts of home and her sleeping family filled her with a flash of emotion—God, how she missed them on night shift. She shrugged her shoulders, shivering at the same time, like a cat shaking off water. Then she attacked the unfinished wheel in the machine with the frenzy of someone who wished to believe her own speed could control the clock.

And finally it was minutes away from midnight. A full moon waited high over the factory roof like a white ball with a golden ring, outshining any stars. Pink lights cast shadows on the path next to the tracks. The entire train yard was a watercolored wash of pink and black. The poem waited with the moon, holding its breath.

The woman was usually the first ready to leave because her locker was in the bathroom of the foreman's office near the door. On other nights she waited to walk to the parking lot with the guys; however, tonight felt different to her as she stepped out ahead of the whistle.

She was short, but her shadow was ten feet tall. She carried a paper sack of dirty work clothes. The poem was with her like another shadow, walking quickly. The farther away she got from the building, the taller her shadow grew, from the yard lights and the moon on her shoulders. Little rocks and pebbles at her feet crunched under her shoes. Each pebble had its own rosy shadow, like pink moon rocks under her feet. She smiled to herself, relishing the moment.

A cat meowed from the path ahead, scurrying away from the woman's flying feet. Stopping abruptly, the cat turned its head to stare back at her, its yellow eyes frozen in black midair. Then it disappeared under a parked freight car.

Night birds called in the distance.

Now her shadow split in two, growing taller, taller, taller. Racing past more pink lights. Stepping nimbly across one, two, three sets of train tracks. Passing flatbed cars stacked with unmachined axles and rows of wheels. Past lines of mounted wheel and axle sets waiting to be shipped out.

A lone crow cawed at her from a telephone wire. Something stirred in her brain. Some disjointed words seemed to come together. She laughed aloud, and the crow cawed again, leaving its perch to soar over her head into the blackness beyond the realm of pink lights. For a fleeting second she saw its dark wings gleam with a blush of pink. Then suddenly the woman threw back her head and shouted up into the pink and black sky. "HEY... I'm a midnight rider. A cat's eye glider. I'm a second shift mother goin' home!"

She laughed again. Surprised and delighted, the poem jumped *inside her* like a fetus kicking in the ninth month. She hurried along, faster now, running the last few yards past the guard shanty.

Finally, she was at her car in the parking lot. She plopped her dirty work clothes on the car hood to pull her keys out of her pocket. She unlocked the door, opened it, and flung the sack into the backseat. Jumping in, she started the car, revved its engine, put the car in gear, and aimed the old '68 Ford out of the lot. She saw the other workers, just then crossing the tracks, waving at her, and she beeped her car horn a couple times in response.

Now she would have time for herself. A smile, glorious as a weekend, spread across her face. She felt the uneasy urgency she'd buried deep inside all night leave her in a great, earthmoving sigh as she drove through the open gate and turned up the road to the ramp leading from the valley.

And a poem was born, comfortable as a well-fitting work shoe, satisfying as the end of the work day. The poem. The woman. The mother. The machinist. All became one. And she sang to the hum of her car:

> *I'm a midnight rider*
> *A cat's eye glider*
> *A second shift mother goin' home.*
>
> *I'm a moon rock walker*
> *A pink bird stalker*
> *A short tall shadow headin' home.*
>
> *I'm a cool old river*
> *A seasoned survivor*
> *I'm a factory workin' poet goin' home.*

MAY 22, 1985

ninety-three days
after the sale
and still
waiting

we are moths
caught
in an oil slick
on the diesel house floor

clouds
of fork truck exhaust
hanging
in midsummer air

old paint flecks
ready to fall off
the damp shop walls
on Mickey
the kid on second shift
who kept on saying
"at least we got a job"
over and over

until the night
he read his name
on the layoff list
and his mouth
clamped shut
tight
as the guard house gate
closing behind him

RED DUST

Davey was a clerk at the railroad
sixteen years union seniority gaining him
a seat outside the bathroom
in the foreman's office
behind a desk smokestacked high with papers

Only Native American in the wheel shop
he tried to bury his identity
for survival in white territory

Became more christian than the christians
to ward off totem pole humor

Carried his bible around for protection
when stepping out into the shop

Just in case he was confronted
with the booming noise of brass hammers
drumming a dubious "tom-tom" beat
on the sides of steel barrels

At least they wouldn't dare a racist joke to his face
when confronted with a sign of the crucifix and
"aw, it's somethin' to do" the guys would say
when I'd ask about intent

Then one afternoon alone together in the office
Davey confided with a conspiratory wink
that he continued to honor his mother's religion
of wind rain and sun in the event
the white man's god fell through

Recounted tales of his childhood on the reservation
his real name Red Dust
his land in northern Wisconsin
settling over graves of friends and relatives
where he returns to hunt with his sons
each Thanksgiving weekend

And the last days before the railroad shut down
saw his bible lying on the desk
gathering dust
closed over a blood-red beaded bookmark

DEFINITIONS

Cheater Bar—"Traditionally male-identified,
mechanical term for a piece of pipe
that can be slid over wrench handles
to obtain greater leverage."

She
didn't appreciate the name.

She wasn't cheating.

Just using her brain.

So she reclaimed it.

Pipe—"An extension of power. Effective.
Persistent. Strong."

Like a woman.

FLOOR DRY

Doc's Story

Doc screws his laborer's hard hat into brillo-pad gray hair. His face is a maze of angular lines. He smiles only when he needs to. Laughs with people he trusts. Tall as a six-foot ladder, his brown-black elbows poke through a red plaid flannel shirt, flared over baggy blue jeans that can't remember blue. Work boots overworked, Doc spends his paycheck on things he deems more important, like betting on horses, the Illinois lottery, and weekends in South Chicago with old friends, close as the family he wishes he had.

Come Monday, Doc slow strides factory aisles behind a wheelbarrow, push broom and long-handled shovel crisscrossed inside. And though not among his assigned laborers' duties, he always manages to find time to check if I need a new bag of floor dry. That's the factory worker's indispensable ally. It looks like kitty litter and absorbs oil spills with thousands of tiny, rocky sponges.

Today Doc spies an almost empty sack propped against the engine lathe. I am one woman in this shop full of men. Only machinist Doc supplies with floor dry, not because he thinks I can't carry it myself, but because he knows how difficult a job I have just being here. Knows, from years of being "one-of-a-kind" himself, starting back in '43, when he was the railroad's only African-American laborer. Seventeen, he was, when the foreman wisecracked, "They'd rather have a white boy for the job, but they were all at war." Doc didn't laugh, he just worked, and his paycheck came every two weeks just like everybody else's.

Doc's other name is Orange Henry. When I ask why, he says it's what they call him in Chicago. Doc and I get along. I give him a hand sweeping up at night and read notices off the bulletin board. (He claims his glasses won't let him see.) Doc breaks up my work day with friendly conversation, laughs with me as he shares a joke when he senses I'm hav-

ing an especially hard day, and gets me floor dry from across
the shop. Lugging it over sets of train tracks with ruts too
deep for wheelbarrows to ride, he yanks a sack off the top of
a three-foot heap and heaves it up and over his left shoulder,
draping the fifty-pound bag around his neck like a collar—
like the fifty, seventy-five, one hundred pounds of railroad
he's been hefting all these years, leaving his body perma-
nently twisted into a bent I-beam.

I watch Doc through a spray of hot metal chips. Waiting
for a long cut to finish on this engine lathe, I'm suddenly
aware of my own body—its weight unevenly distributed,
left hip sticking out like one crooked axle protruding from
the center of a pile.

As Doc trudges towards me, bobbing up and down as if his
left foot were stepping in a series of holes, I straighten up,
stretch my arms to the arched ceiling where the railroad
pigeons live. I put my arms to my sides, pull my shoulders
down and back, and plant my legs wide apart for balance
until the machine is done cutting and I can reach my little
wooden crate to rest one foot up on as I know I should.

And here comes Doc leaning over to plop the floor dry
down in a spew of flying, granulated dust. Even from this
stooped-over stance his hard hat never retreats from grooves
machined in his hair line. I yell THANKS, watching his
strong frame unbend in time-lapse photography. Doc doesn't
say a word, just gives a work-gloved wave, smiles straight at
me, and moves on.

TWO FOR MENOPAUSE

ONE

flash

hot face
spinning iron
ears burning
heart pounding
mouth dry
scalp itching under my hard hat
sweat dripping down my cheeks
safety glasses sliding off my nose
trying to get the last damn axle of the day
cut and on its way
in the middle of a heavy hot flash
and here comes my friend Earl
from the machine next door
zipping up his jacket
to ward off forty degree indoor
winter factory wind chills
he gives a knowing grin
and motions me to sit down
on the overturned barrel
behind the lathe
while he takes over to finish the job
    as for me
     i don't say no

TWO

at night

the hormones wake
to dance and party
naked in the rain

i try to tell them
shut up
i gotta get some sleep
i gotta go to work tomorrow
for pete's sake
shut the racket down
but they don't listen
they set fire to my feet
and pour buckets of rainwater
all over my body
except my feet
which by now
feel like fried sausages
sticking out of wet
fuzzy blanket buns
so what's a woman
supposed to do
but get up outa bed

and dance

VERONA, YOUR LIFE

is a victory
and your story should be told,
how your blue collar work began
at the railroad in Milwaukee
at the end of the Second World War.

You'd been a waitress in the cafeteria
till it shut down after the men came home.
Not much sense, but that's the railroad.

The waitresses were told to make a choice:
become laborers, or quit.
Some of them tried. One of them stayed.
Who said the war was over?
You fought a battle every day they didn't want you there.
And that was every day you worked.

The foreman had you hauling rocks in a wheelbarrow
from one pile to another,
to make you tired,
to make you give up.
Instead *they* got tired of watching.

You were a "Rosie the Riveter" who would not go away.
You raised your kids on railroad wages,
grew your muscles strong as the sturdy plants
on your Wisconsin window sill,
your life full as your wheelbarrow,
your smile long as your seniority,
and I was proud to work with you those last few years,
even if we were on opposite shifts.

You came to work a little early.
I stayed a little late, and
our shifts meshed like a set of perfect gear teeth.

Until the railroad was sold
and our jobs derailed like a train wreck.
It seems another war was over without a bullet ever fired.
I knew I'd be out the door but
thought there might be hope for you.

Then the bulletin board did the dirty work.
You'd been laid off
with less than a year to go till retirement.
They wouldn't let you work your remaining days
in the wheel shop
even though it was to stay open for some time.
They wanted only one laborer,
and he had more whiskers in the union,

and he was a he.

"But, hey, here's a deal!" they said.
You could sell the home where you raised your family.
Leave your grown children, friends, and grandchildren
and move to Minneapolis for a job of unknown merits.

You said,
"NO"
and retired at sixty
with a pocket full of severance pay and your family
at your side.

After all, this wasn't the first time
the railroad demanded that you make a choice,
and your decision was right

both times.

HARD TIMES IN THE VALLEY

one day at a time they tell us
well that's fine for a tv comedy show
but no way to plan a life

jobs hanging on
i don't knows/maybes
and bathroom rumors of transfers
to Chicago or Minneapolis

we deserve more than five days' notice
on the bulletin board before
they yank us out of our boots
without unlacing them

we are the guts
the muscle of this railroad
we know how to run machines
that have long since passed their prime
how to create singing axles and wheels
out of mute steel

we gave 10/20/30 years to this place
came in every day to keep the railroad going
obligated to quality
safety
commitment
to babies mothers fathers
grain and toothbrushes riding on our work

now all we know for sure
is no damn paycheck pays enough
for these hard times in the valley

WHITE COLLAR CRIME

new owners' "reps" skulk through the plant
like hyenas panting for meat
each day a new pack
measuring our legs and production slips
drooling in anticipation
for the end of a ninety-day court-ordered wait

new owners want the place cleaned up
Soo Line has white walls they say
ours underneath the grease and flaking grime
are gray
we think

new owners rob us of our weekends
worry bites holes into Friday night plans
now they steal
our makeshift factory furniture
empty wire spools for tables
overturned oil barrel chairs with taped-on cushions
wooden crate footstools
all gone

but we fight back
at breaktime spread clean shop rags
on the flat parts of machines
turn off their electric switch boxes
open our lunch bags
and perch
like birds on telephone wires
before a storm

SHOP HUMOR

anonymous cartoon appears
is quickly copied at lunchtime
on the machine in the main shop office
flies like smoke from a diesel
traveling at ninety miles per hour
decorating tool benches
lunch tables
passed hand to hand
contagious as a smile
day before a holiday

american eagle labeled SOO LINE
taking up the whole page
wings spread talons extended
bearing down on a little grinning mouse
MILWAUKEE ROAD signing its t-shirt
holding a clenched paw up to the eagle
middle finger pointed straight in the air

LAST GREAT ACT OF DEFIANCE
reads the caption

anything to get us through
another dreaded day

Talkin' Union

ONE Oil

Spotting two committeemen walking up the aisle, I toss the
magazine I'm reading on the tool bench, and finish the end of
a long cut on the axle in the journal lathe. I back off the tool
and turn down the speed and feed, still keeping the axle spin-
ning in the machine. Then I wave my arms at the union reps
like one of those signal corps people on an aircraft carrier.

Now, understand that every male who passes through this
shop on his way to somewhere else usually stares over at
number eight machine. It's the journal lathe standing right at
the main doorway. The one that the only female machinist
at the railroad runs. Maybe they want to watch her actually
making train axles and getting dirty. Maybe they never saw a
female machinist before. Maybe they think they'll see more
than some short person wearing loose overalls and a red ban-
dana underneath her green hard hat operating a journal
lathe. Call it male curiosity or whatever you want, but it hap-
pens every time.

So when these guys pretend *not* to see me flapping shop
rags in the air, I *know* what they're doing. Earl does too, next
door to me on another lathe. Earl was the second African-
American machinist on the Milwaukee Road in 1965.
Emmett was the first, some time in the fifties, but he's
retired now. Emmett went to most of the union meetings.
Earl goes when it's contract time, but he says they never lis-
ten to him, so why bother. I try to convince him that it
always pays to bother, and then we go round and round like
the axles in the machines we run.

The committeemen are almost to the doorway when Earl
shouts HEY loud enough to be heard above the factory noise

and comes out from behind the fifteen-foot-long machine. Little blue curls of steel chips fly off the axle he's cutting to size. They hit his hard hat with a clicking sound of popcorn popping in a pan. Now he's standing right in front of the reps out of chip range. He doesn't say another word, just points his work-gloved index finger towards me and my shop rags. Earl walks back to tend to his machining. The committeemen walk cautiously toward my direction looking like they expect me to stuff them into the lathe with the spinning axle. They begin speaking before I open my mouth to ask a question.

WE DON'T KNOW ANYTHING.
WE HAVEN'T HEARD ANYTHING.
WE CAN'T SAY ANYTHING.

Undaunted, I ask anyway. WHAT HAPPENED AT THE MEETING IN CHICAGO LAST WEEK? WHAT ABOUT OUR SEVERANCE PAY? HOW MANY MORE LAYOFFS?

And they hurry off before I finish my last question, not even turning around to look at me when they repeat with the emphasis of a slamming toolbox lid: WE DON'T KNOW ANYTHING.

Earl walks over shaking his head side to side and mumbles, "We don't have a union. We'll see it on TV before they tell us."

I sigh, wanting to believe he's not right, but today I'm tired of responding with my usual "it's better than nothing" arguments.

I feel like an empty oil barrel trying to remember oil in another time, another factory.

It was the small shop where I got my first machinist job. There was no union to defend or blame. No contract to complain about. I watched the owner stalk his aisles each morning making employment decisions that changed people's lives with a tap on their shoulder. Someone could be fired with ten years at the same machine and there was no recourse. No such thing as "seniority rights." People were afraid to talk, even at lunchtime. Men of color and women of any ethnicity were the usual targets, but no one was safe from the shoulder tap. Nothing to be done but fold up your canvas apron and go home.

I start another cut on the lathe and reach for my magazine, *Talkin' Union*. I glance over at Earl. He's reading the copy I gave him yesterday. The machine in front of him is cutting air.

I guess there's always a drop of oil left in the bottom of a barrel.

TWO Conversations

union official from national headquarters
attends a local monthly meeting

our dues pay his salary but
this is the first time we've seen his face
here to tell us we can't do anything
about the new contract
he's sorry but it's out of his hands
We Can Strike we say

No Use he says

Got Nothin' To Lose we say

You'll Lose Your Jobs he says

We Lost 'Em Anyway we say
The Place Is Shutting Down

official shrugs his shoulders
looks at the floor
stares at the ceiling
clears his throat
gathers and stacks his papers in a pile

we yell
he yells
we yell
he leaves
we leave and
somewhere the people who own it all
sit smiling dollar signs

WORKIN' ON YEAR TWELVE

went to work today
satisfied with seven pretty fine axles
journals with perfect three-degree angles
microfinish shiny tens
passed by Sylvester the inspector's
jeweler's eye
ate a lunch packed by my honey
with a love note under the apple
to remind me I'm on his mind
right that minute
was left alone
by foremen/supervisors
and the guy who sees flying saucers
wasn't left alone
by my good shop buddies
didn't want to escape
on vacation or weekend
and it wasn't even payday
it was just a Tuesday
workin' on year twelve

PICTURE OF A BACKWARD WORKER

Willard Plumerson was dead before his time
    but he was born again
    in a burst of economic paranoia
    heaven and white skin privilege
    holding more promise
    than his sliding stock quotations

he kept busy
    scurrying to the foreman's office
    to tattle on other workers' toilet activities
    in between cutting train axles
    on an engine lathe he called his own
    for over forty years

Willard made few friends
    with his boasts of blue chip stocks
    had no friends for support
    when they plummeted sometime in the '60s
    in a smoldering heap
    like the trash tray's steel fragments
    in the belly of the lathe

he couldn't quite find his class
    not "working"
    not "middle"
    he floated somewhere on a republican cloud
    with his white jesus
    and a micrometer
    that was always at least
    three thousandths of an inch
    away from accurate

he couldn't quite place his heart
    not "management"
    not "union"
    his only seat on a board
    was the one behind the lathe
    where he'd eat his lunch alone
    or on special occasions
    with a couple others just as scared as he

there they'd argue the body count
    of angels dancing on the heads of pins
    out of bibles on their blue-jeaned laps
    where bankruptcy
    plant closures
    and quality circle lies
    were never listed as realities of life

FACTS

Dedicated to my sister Tradeswomen

somewhere between days when we can't find anything good to say
about being a woman in a blue collar job and
the times when we feel like Amazons is
the fact of getting up to go to work each day
every day at five in the morning winter dark Wisconsin
snow covering the goddamn car
dig the stupid thing out so you can go to work
where you know there'll be ice on the steel axles and wheels you're
supposed to machine and the ice will fly off in chunks
and hit your hard hat and make you glad you have it on for once
not like in the summer when it's so hot the micrometer readings
aren't accurate and you just want to go to the beach and
lie all day like a fig or a tobacco leaf or a peach
and the fact is it's work to go to work and
harder when you get there and harder yet
when you're the only woman and you're forced to
make careful daily decisions including
even the clothes you wear
like pants that don't show this or that and
baggy shirts to cover your tits and that's the way it is
if you want to make some money
to support yourself and your family
legally in this society and you're a woman and you're working
in a factory or on a dock or a construction site and
the other people that work there are men

and you start to feel your power your muscles in your arms
in your legs it feels good and you don't take crap from anyone
and the nice guys are nice
the shitty guys are shitty
the ones in between are nice some days and not nice other days
and then there's some who are never nice
who are awful who want you gone or dead but for sure not there
but the money is good is necessary
and you learn to keep the boss away
and the shitty and awful guys away
and the nice guys even help
once in a while and you make friends more than enemies
and you teach every day every day and you learn
how to do your job better than all of them
because you have to just to stay equal whatever that means
and you rush around forever trying to keep
on your steel-booted toes
getting very very very tired
and that's a fact

SUBJECT TO CHANGE

Hump Day, Wednesday, midafternoon, and it's another meeting in the Milwaukee Road back shop. Nothing there but empty aisles since bankruptcy court erased jobs clear as a Sunday A.M. parking lot. No machinery screams, roars, and squeals. No bright orange and black locomotives balanced over maintenance pits. No overhead crane cabs swaying and clacking on their rails. The only sounds bounding off cracked cement walls are the murmurs of our own voices mingling with flapping whirs and coos of pigeons in the wooden beams high above us.

And here we stand, hands in overalled pockets, curious eyes counting numbers against another layoff clock. Green, red, blue, and gold hard hats dot the crowd, depending on each individual shop craft. They are the only colors of life from a pigeon's-eye view. The work-dirty hats are askew, tilted purposefully at disrespectful angles to greet management "reps" when they arrive.

Near as we can tell, there's about 150 of us gathered under the unpatched roof of this century-old building. And we're all waiting. The building itself, ancient history to the bankruptcy judge, is scheduled for demolition in the coming months. The employees, futures less reliable, shift from one steel-toed boot to another, centered in this particular moment of waiting.

We have lost count of these assemblies. They're not worth getting out of work to attend. We'd rather be back at the machines, producing something tangible.

And here come the company men down the aisle. Six of them in business suits topped off by spotless white hard hats, like a row of snowballs in summer. I automatically shiver. The guy next to me stuffs his hands in his pockets. We watch these men with the nervous anticipation of patients waiting in a surgeon's office. And yet we know they won't know all the answers. They aren't the owners, or even the ones who sit at the board meetings. We know it. They know it. They have a job as long as we do. Their faces are strained. Smiles forced. They stop several feet away from the first row of blue collar employees as if there were an invisible line drawn in the concrete floor.

Slanted afternoon sun rays arc from broken ceiling windows to spotlight the scene. Particles of dust and pigeon feathers are pushed up/down in drafts of air blowing in through the over-head doorway. The movie-screen-wide doors gape open to view the end of Wisconsin summer in the Menomonee River industrial valley. Brown clumps of weeds toss in the breeze. Idle forklift trucks grip empty pallets in their teeth. Stacks of miscellaneous diesel engine parts are tagged in metal bins waiting for some place to go. A wrecking ball dangling from a tractor crane cable is not swayed by the wind.

A snowball coughs. Another wipes his glasses on a hand-kerchief, white as the papers he caresses protectively under his arm. The meeting begins. The sounds of their voices swirl in the air with pigeon dirt. What tiny hope we might have had is lost in phrases like: "maybe next month . . . could be travel package . . . some layoffs . . . can't be sure how many . . . some relocation . . . can't be sure when . . . but of course it's all subject to change." Meaningless sentences bombard our hard hats like bird shit. A pigeon flies out the door.

"Are there any questions?" asks a snowball.

"Sure," comes an anonymous wisecrack from the captured audience, "but you won't give us any straight answers."

And it's another meeting to leave, feeling helpless as the tumbling weeds rolling 'cross the train tracks. We are unusu-ally quiet as we make our way back to finish our shift. The bankruptcy court decree has completed another one of its duties. Produced a perfunctory meeting, directed by a right-wing Illinois judge who has known contacts with organized crime. Our intelligence has been insulted. We are victims of a criminal act. Pieces of reality left behind.

Positive that we are the only things left alive in this dying valley, we begin to shout, push, shove each other like school kids outside at a fire drill. We are a blue-jeaned parade without a crowd in the reviewing stand. Anger pulls our boots to kick at passing weeds. Rocks take to the air, ricocheting off side-tracked box cars. Blushes of adrenaline that raged in our veins at the meeting surface to explode in a sort of crazed humor.

Eddie takes a baseball pitcher's stance, and flings a rusty bolt at a tin shed. Then he says, "Just might make a car payment this month." (They sent him two late notices.) "Course," he pauses with a sarcastic grin, "it's subject to change."

Earl winks, immediately playing along, "Tonight for sure, I'm goin' right home after work." He clears his throat dramatically, "Then again, it *could be* subject to change."

We laugh together. It feels good.

I throw a large gray rock at a puddle several yards away. It lands on its mark with a good splash and I yell, "Hey! I hear there's five new machinists coming tomorrow. All women! But maybe that's subject to change too!"

And we march along, releasing frustration with each step. Our procession shrinks in size as people enter buildings along the way. The wheel shop gang is the last to reach its destination. We experience a communal surge of relief to be back on familiar ground and away from the sight of a wrecking ball. Inside, the machines have been waiting. Patient green monsters with sleeping jaws. We walk the last few steps to our separate work areas, then, one at a time, awaken each monster with the vengeance of dictators. The air compressor blasts. Cranes clatter. Engine lathes, boring-bars, mills, drills, and forklifts rumble and growl, till the football-field-sized factory is a comforting roar, loud enough to silence the sound of our futures, subject to change.

42

COFFEE CLUB

this is the morning coffee club
regrouping like soldiers losing comrades in a battle

these are the over-sixty veterans
holding off retirement until the last wheel and axle set
goes rolling out the doors
these are railroad machinists
collecting forty years of memories and seniority
as they sit and lean on counters in the bearing room

they belong to the railroad
as much as the stacks of rings, seals,
and dark brown, train bearing cups that surround them
as they drink their coffee
read newspapers
tell jokes
and count the younger guys
who've left for yards in Minnesota
where the railroad's new owners claim to keep them working

clustered in the bearing room
they avoid the bankrupt horror of the outer shop
where silent machines stand like scratched green statues
before they're reassigned or sold

journey level in hiding their emotions
tightly gripping steaming mugs as if they too will disappear
inside each man is an old bull huddled in a barn
trying to withstand the winter wind crying through the cracks

EVERYTHING CHANGES

In '41 there were three women bolt cutters
at the Milwaukee Road machine shops
in the Menomonee River Valley
underneath the 35th Street viaduct

There was a women's bathroom
in the wheel shop
for the bolt cutters
one in the back shop for the laborer
that cleaned the offices
and another in the warehouse
for the female clerks

Then World War II ended
and the men that were left alive
came home to the women in the factories
being swept away
with the last shift's steel chips
and their bathrooms were converted to
storerooms
and men's locker space
(men of color segregated from white,
of course)
and the women went home
to have the babies
that died in the Vietnam War

Then in 1978
thanks to the civil rights
and women's movements
(and a fire of unexplained origin
that burned down
the old locker shed in the sixties)

the segregated lockers
had been integrated
six females were hired
two welders
one machinist's helper
one laborer
one machine apprentice
and one machinist
to work with the 600
male employees in the valley
with one less toilet
for the women to pee in
than their sisters had in the forties

In 1985
after bankruptcy
reorganization
broken promises
lies and layoffs
there were two factory women
left at the "road"
the laborer that survived
the Second World War
and me
both of us sharing a bathroom
with two foremen
one male clerk
and whatever men
walk in and out of the office
proving once again
that progress
is not the same
as revolution

46

POEM FOR THE EX-MILWAUKEE ROAD GANG

relocated
alone in Minnesota
Wisconsin born
small town rooted
suspicious of change like any good Milwaukeean
dumped in Minneapolis Central Avenue Yards
like a load of foreign freight wheels
pretending courage to each other
as they command strange tools to fit their hands
until the shift is through
and they can drink some time away
in someone else's neighborhood tavern

HERE'S ONE FOR THE SOO LINE CREW

railroad in their souls
same as Milwaukee Roaders
tired blood red eyes
Soo Line second shifters
smirk at the foremen's backs
smile and bullshit each other
muscling their hammers and air guns
driving bolts in and out of boxcar frames
cutting torches sparking red hot dots of burning steel
working hands guts and hearts
for a paycheck every fifteen days

KITTENS

Victories are kittens
to be celebrated with a cheer
for each tiny meow handed up from the pit
beneath the wheel mounting press,
production stopped before day shift whistled it in.
Kittens birth-dropped by a mamma shop cat,
in a nice dark place she thought was safe,
sometime over the weekend.
But how was she to know the wheel press is a machine
whose job is scrunching train wheels onto axles,
with an average 160 tons of pressure.

And it was Eddie of the mounting gang
who first heard their newborn squeaks.
Didn't want to start the day with mashed cats,
anyway it was Monday.
So he gathered the morning coffee group around,
and they all agreed, "We gotta get 'em out."
Went and told the foreman, "Can't work.
Somethin's in the press."

Then one by one, tiny fur balls
in hands bigger than three kittens put together,
were passed into a bearing box lined with clean rags,
and relocated to the back shop,
emptied months ago
by bankruptcy court decree.

Small survivors of displacement.
Kittens transported in a forklift
driven slow and easy for a change,
gentle over railroad tracks and potholes
in the graveled roads.
Victories alive.

Like John the machinist, two years later,
working again after the final shutdown
of all Milwaukee Road facilities, running the same machine
he made diesel wheels on for twenty-five years
before different owners tore it out of the valley floor
and transplanted it in a new wheel shop's cement.
No union. Less money.
But, "Hey, ya gotta roll with the punches.
It's a job until retirement."

Earl's there too, running old number seven axle lathe
after a year fighting third shift traffic
Milwaukee to Chicago, where the ones who bought the railroad
threw some jobs.

Soo Line didn't throw anything Eddie's way.
He's at the post office and better off he says.
The mounting press and its white lead paint's
a disaster to store with Agent Orange from Vietnam.

Don the Union president's retired.
So's the Union. It closed its books,
gave a party, and donated its bank balance
to a place that trains Seeing Eye dogs.
Don's in his backyard come springtime
figuring out ways to keep squirrels
out of the bird feeder he built.
Don takes fishing trips up north
and keeps house waiting for his wife
to join him in retirement.
We hear he made a surprise visit to the new wheel shop
talking to old friends.

Had the foremen and supervisors running around looking worried.
Seems Don was wearing his belt buckle
with the two-inch high machinists union crest.
Don just smiled. Each day's a gift since bypass surgery.

Verona, the only female laborer, has retired too,
a forty-year veteran of more than one battle.
A grandmother with never enough time for herself,
she's still taking care of people,
her laborer's heart and hands cleaning up their lives,
sorting out her own.
Grabbing on to precious hours to attend quilting classes
or take long slow walks in the woods whenever she wants,
now time sits on her windowsill, waiting for *her* to tell it what to do.

Then there's Sue. First woman machinist on the railroad,
in its hundred-year history.
Stayed in the trade for over twelve years.
Nobody thought she could do it.
Thirty-seven by the time she even started.
"A female," they said. "Too short," they said.
To top it off, she had five kids at home.
She'll be absent all the time.

They were wrong.
Sue earned her retirement from machining the hard way.
Hung up her micrometer, and in the end
got some of that union-won severance pay
everyone was talking about.
Kids grown up and on their own,
Sue moved to California with her best friend,
her second husband. And in the middle of menopause
for goodness sake!

And don't you know, the wheel shop gang still communicates,
trading tales like numbers on production slips.
Shouting from one end of the country to the other,
WE'RE STILL HERE. WE'RE OKAY.
Like kittens from the mounting press,
survival's a victory to be counted.

THE JOB SEARCH 1986

ONE Food

looking for work in California
is more difficult
is the same
is less difficult
is looking for work in sunshine
instead of snow

and the jobs elude us
hide behind sunspots
college degrees and journey cards that
were never received

and people are nice
are not nice
and they say that we will find work
eventually
just be patient

and we are
patient
while we count
our disappearing canned goods
wondering who we could ask
for a loan
maybe someone
who wouldn't make us feel
that we should have stayed put
in Wisconsin
like middle-aged people ought to
for heaven's sake

then I really get a job
or I think it's a job
even though it isn't the best
and it's a non-union machine shop
with three young guys
and a speedy foreman who doesn't act too pleased
with my being hired
by the woman boss who thinks I'm
interesting

and I'm working in this place for two days
and they don't believe in breaks
and the lunchroom is a sidewalk outside
where I sit alone on a little foam rubber square
found in a pile behind the engine lathe
they tell me to run
but it's okay because it's ten bucks an hour
and the engine lathe is old
but interesting

and it's the second day in the afternoon
and I'm sure of the machine
cutting cast iron smooth as gray butter
to plus or minus one thousandth of an inch
after centering each piece perfectly
in a four jaw chuck and I'm tired but happy
about a paycheck coming at the end of the week
when suddenly out of the blue California sky
the foreman runs up to me and yells
he doesn't want to train me anymore
and I think to myself all he ever did
was point to this lathe yesterday
and tell me where the cast iron pieces were

oh, I forgot I had to ask him for the blueprint
maybe that was the training part

anyway, I hadn't even seen him all day
been working fine alone
while my three coworkers were busy
breaking blades on the band saw
jamming cutters into brass
and screwing up hundreds of dollars of copper
and I was just going to go find the foreman
to ask what to do next because my work was finished
when he told me my work was really finished
so I didn't get a job anyway
but the woman boss gave me a ride home
with my toolbox and that was sisterly I guess
or at least
interesting

TWO Clothing

dressing up for the office temporaries
I wear my black slacks
my only pair of slacks
all my other pants are blue jeans
but the job counselor said
that blue jeans
aren't what I'm supposed to wear
to look for work in the temporaries

performing typing tests typing
57 words per minute but they subtract 2
for each mistake and I have 9 mistakes so
I don't type 57 words per minute
and my typing speed isn't good
isn't good enough to be a typist
in the temporaries

my black slacks are sweaty now
I sit on a plastic chair
taking another test
adding subtracting dividing
multiplying and spelling
showing my best handwriting that isn't my best
because I'm so nervous my hand shakes
causing my handwriting to look like spa-gh-it-ti
and I can't spell spaghetti either
and the temporary woman says
don't worry I can register as
light industry and receptionist

maybe I could be a receptionist
in light industry
industry of lights
industry of sunlight
California sunshine industry

maybe I could sit outside
in the California sunshine
and receive it
wouldn't that be a receptionist

to hell with the typing anyway

THREE Shelter

the temporary woman told me to call every day
and they'd tell me if they have a job for me

now it's two weeks later and I've called every day
even the two days when I thought
I had the machine shop job
and I didn't

two weeks later
and I still haven't been placed anyplace
permanent or temporary

but it's California
and we live here

and it really is
sunny

BICYCLES AND OTHER MACHINES 1986

I'll never forget how to ride a bike
it was 1943 on my brother's two-wheeler
balloon tire Schwinn navy blue bike frame
manufactured of pre-World War II steel
when I taught myself to get on with one foot
on the cement steps by the sidewalk
in front of our house
figured how to dismount
by falling over on purpose
bike and all
onto the green curve
of the lawn hill so's not to ram the crossbar
in my six-year-old crotch
still remember the glorious ride
and the pain
of learning the hard way

these days I ride on subway trains
and pass by crews of Oakland factory workers
on breaks at 8 A.M. as I commute to an office job

catch glimpses out the window of men
perched on upturned barrels and wire-spool tables
dunking donuts in steaming mugs and dented thermos cups
smell the coffee in their bear paw hands
feel the splintered wood as if it were beneath
my own fanny instead of this train car cushion
hear their shits and damnits as the factory
whistles them inside to hammers and machines
sniff the shop odor of oil and diesel smoke
see my hand holding the pen
as I write this all down

knuckles scarred with tiny jagged lines and ridges
where hot steel chips cut flesh
like flesh in another life on a different job
made me bury pain deep in my brain
under my hard hat so I could do the work
society says is for a man
so I try to bury my feelings like the men
and try to become a different kind of woman

try to blend in try not to take the hardness home with me
the stubbornness that I need to survive
I don't need at home
but it's difficult to put away
because I'll need it the next day

to be working with the men again who think
and say right to my face that I'm taking the place
of their son or kid brother taking Joe or Al or Fred's job away
sure I must be
should be home taking care of kids
barefoot and pregnant or at least washing clothes
or dishes or porch steps or something
washing something getting it clean
like a woman's supposed to and not getting dirty
learning the hard way for chrissake
I'll never forget the ride

SI SE PUEDE

Transition poems especially for Jesusita

ONE The Electrician

golden hawk
electric as the universe
searching California hills
for perfect currents
to keep herself aloft

time is as precious
as the inhabitants
of her nest below
it is the air on which she soars
she does not waste a breath of it

purposefully gliding earthward
sparks crackling talons against stone
she lands
gripping the side of a mountain
as if she owns it

when change ruffles her feathers
like a fierce sudden wind
her flight pattern adjusts
always herself
Jesusita
a golden hawk
at one with the sky

and a hawk must fly

TWO The Counselor

listens to herself
timing is most important
she says

realizing the precise moment
when wind becomes flight
can be done

63

BLUE COLLAR GOODBYES

blue collar goodbyes are a jumpstart
on a frozen battery midnight parking lot
peering out of second shift propped open coffee eyes
wide as inch-and-a-quarter sockets
from a toolbox back at the radial drill machine
in Allis Chalmers Tractor Shop
where the only African-American on the housing line
teams up with the only female in maintenance repair
to move those tractors out the door

now Bill Dunlap's powerful hands fasten jumper cables
to plus and minus inside car hoods exposed to winter in Wisconsin
my '71 Ford and Bill's bran' new step-up van's competent motor
vibrating powdered snow like sifted cake flour
off a gleaming waxed finish revealing
Bill's stencil painted signature design
DADDY HIGH POCKETS
and his wife Bernice's
LADY LOW POCKETS
in the cold moon glow blue brightness

as my engine finally turns over
warming up goodbyes satisfying
as Bill and Bernice's faces across their kitchen table
heavy with platters of deep Southern-fried catfish
and hot cornbread put out for company
my home partner Larry and I over for Saturday night

and Bill waits inside his van to be sure
I'm not stuck in ice ruts
then fifteen years and a plant closure later
Bill's gone
I'm gone
Allis Chalmers is gone

blue collar goodbyes become letters and phone calls
from back home Bill and Bernice
and Milwaukee Road buddies Earl, Don, and Verona
veterans of yet another plant closing down, another buyout
by a hungrier corporation
another selling out up the hill
with nothing but our lunch buckets
more forced layoffs, a few paid severances,
don't know how many transfers to Chicago or Minneapolis
where the Soo Line promised jobs then
four years later about to go belly up too,
it offers those same people a chance to buy
their own failing railroad
in a town they never wanted to live in
blue collar goodbyes report Wisconsin to California
on lined school notebook paper stark and strong
THERE'S BACK PAY COMING...YOU BETTER CALL
and phoning find the Soo Line
would've kept my blood-earned money
if I had not been told

if I had not known
the hearts of survivors
that corporate minds will never know

survivors of shutdowns and forty-below-zero wind chills
work friends like family separated
by job change and cross-country miles
people who hold dear and remember lunch buckets
Saturday catfish and goin' home car rides that never say never
'cause we'll see you sometime
goodbyes like sparks of electricity through jumper cables
in a midnight parking lot

TRADESWOMEN

you welcome me
with calloused hands
embrace me
with arms that developed
muscles for survival
as well as strength
show me confidence
with eyes that shout
IT CAN BE DONE
reach out with
that quick friendship
learned from necessity
as i offer you
a sister tradeswoman
twelve years plus
of machinist micrometer
readings right on the money
excitement as real
as flying hot metal chips
smiles of satisfaction
of a job well done
i offer you
twelve years plus
of grit and grief
and the loneliness
that only those who are
the First and Only ones
can know

i offer you
a kinship based
on our mutual needs
and wants i want
to learn this job
as carefully as
the engine lathe
in my first training class
as quickly as we find
the only other woman
we hear is on a job site
as loving as we women
can be i offer you
this upraised
calloused fist
matched to yours
when opened shows
our jobs well done

OTHER SOURCES

Plant Closure/Layoff/Stress Information

The Center for Economic Conversion, founded in 1975, is a nonprofit benefit corporation dedicated to building a sustainable peace-oriented economy. Write to the Center for Economic Conversion, 222 View Street, Suite C, Mountain View CA 94041, (415) 968-8798. Ask about their magazine, *Positive Alternatives*.

The Center for Working Life is a mental health counseling program concentrating on problems arising from work stress, plant closure, blue or white collar layoff or termination trauma in the California Bay Area. For information, contact the Center for Working Life, 600 Grand Avenue, Suite 305, Oakland CA 94610, (510) 893-7343. Also ask about seminars and training sessions in cities outside California.

The Federation for Industrial Retention and Renewal is a clearing-house for information concerning support and/or advocacy and action organizations for workers in plant closure situations. Write for data about organizations/assistance in your locality. Contact FIRR, 3411 West Diversey Avenue, #10, Chicago IL 60647, (312) 252-7676.

Jobs with Peace is a grass roots membership organization that works to redirect government spending away from the military and toward domestic concerns. A diverse, multiracial group, Jobs with Peace empowers the socially and economically disadvantaged through participation in the political process. In the Milwaukee area, write for information to Jobs with Peace, 4417 West North Avenue, Milwaukee WI 53208, (414) 444-6010. Also ask about their monthly newspaper, *The Milwaukee Advocate*. For information about Jobs with Peace chapters in your area, contact: National Jobs with Peace Headquarters, 76 Summers Street, Boston MA 02110.

The Labor Heritage Foundation is a national organization dedicated to raising the awareness of workers' culture within the labor movement and among the general public. For more information, contact the Labor Heritage Foundation, 815 16th Street NW, Room 301, Washington D.C. 20006, (202) 842-7880.

The Plant Closures Project is a labor-religious-community alliance based in Oakland. Formed in 1981, the project helps workers and communities fight plant closures, educates the public about economic dislocation, and participates in statewide, national, and international efforts to develop and implement democratic and just economic policies. The Plant Closures Project is located at 518 17th Street, Oakland CA 94612, (510) 763-6584.

Worker Writer Books and Publications

These authors touch our daily working lives. Their "new work writing" takes as its theme the accurate portrayal of how we feel as we try to find jobs, deal with contemptuous bosses, celebrate our first paychecks, try to find fleeting moments of empowerment, and generally try to get through each day without going crazy.

Brodine, Karen. *Woman Sitting at the Machine, Thinking.* Red Letter Press, 409 Maynard Avenue South, #201, Seattle WA 98104.

Butters, Chris. *Propaganda of a Seed.* Cardinal Press, 76 Yorktown, Tulsa OK 94110.

Daniels, Jim. *Punching Out.* Wayne State University Press, Leonard N. Simons Building, 5959 Woodward Avenue, Detroit MI 48202.

70

Doro, Sue. *Heart, Home and Hard Hats*. Midwest Villages and Voices, 3220 10th Avenue South, Minneapolis MN 55407. (For bulk rates of ten or more copies for adult literacy, labor studies, English as a second language, or other classroom use, contact Working People Press, 485 Wesley Avenue, #4, Oakland CA 94606.)

Eisenberg, Susan. *It's a Good Thing I'm Not Macho*. Whetstone Press, 245 Pelham Road, Amherst MA 01002.

Eisenberg, Susan, ed. *Coffee Break Secrets*. Word of Mouth Productions, 9 Rockview Street, Jamaica Plain MA 02130. (Also available on videocassette as a multimedia performance by worker writers who reflect a cross section of occupations.)

Evans, Larry, ed. *Overtime*. Piece of the Hunk Publishers/ West End Press, 319 Clearview Avenue, Pittsburgh PA 15205.

Hass, Gilda. *Plant Closures: Myths, Realities and Responses*. South End Press, 116 St. Botolph Street, Boston MA 02115.

Labor Notes. 7435 Michigan Avenue, Detroit MI 48210.

Le Sueur, Meridel. *Worker Writers*. West End Press, Box 27334, Albuquerque NM 87125.

Martin, Molly, ed. *Hard-Hatted Women: Stories of Struggle and Success in the Trades*. Seal Press, Box 13, Seattle WA 98111.

Martz, Sandra, ed. *If I Had a Hammer: Women's Work in Poetry, Fiction, and Photographs.* Papier-Mache Press, 795 Via Manzana, Watsonville CA 95076-9154.

Talkin' Union. (Back issues available.) Saul Schniderman, Box 5349, Takoma Park MD 20912.

Tradeswomen Magazine. Tradeswomen, Inc., Box 40664, San Francisco CA 94140.

Villani, Jim, and Naton Leslie, eds. *Labor and the Post-Industrial Age.* Pig Iron Press, Box 237, Youngstown OH 44501.

Wayman, Tom. *Going for Coffee—Poetry on the Job.* Harbour Publishing Co. Ltd., Box 219, Madeira Park BC, Canada V0N 2H0. (Also ask your bookstore about other books authored and edited by Tom Wayman, including *Free Time, Waiting for Wayman, Money and Rain, Living on the Ground, A Planet Mostly Sea, Inside Job—Essays on the New Work Writing,* and *Paper Work.*)

Wolf, Lisa. *Womansong.* (Audiocassette.) 344 8th Street, #2, Ann Arbor MI 48103.

Wong, Nellie. *The Death of Long Steam Lady.* West End Press, Box 27334, Albuquerque NM 87125.

Working Classics. (Back issues available.) David Joseph, 298 9th Avenue, San Francisco CA 94118.

Zandy, Janet, ed. *Calling Home: Working Class Women's Writings.* Rutgers University Press, 109 Church Street, New Brunswick NJ 08901.

ABOUT THE AUTHOR

Sue Doro is a worker writer who lives in Oakland, California. She was, for nearly thirteen years, the only female machinist for the Milwaukee Road Railway, as well as a maintenance machinist in the Allis Chalmers Corporation Tractor Shop in Milwaukee, Wisconsin. *Blue Collar Goodbyes* is based on her experiences at the railroad during its bankruptcy, buy out, and closure—events that strongly effected the lives of employees and their families.

After the closing of the railway, Doro came to California to serve for two and a half years as the Executive Director for Tradeswomen, Inc., a national membership support and advocacy organization for women in blue collar "new traditional" jobs. She is currently employed as an affirmative action compliance officer for the U.S. Department of Labor. She continues to serve as Poetry Editor for *Tradeswomen Magazine.*

Sue Doro is married to Larry Robbin, and is the mother of five children. She has two previously published collections: *Heart, Home and Hard Hats* (1986, Midwest Villages and Voices) and *Of Birds and Factories* (1983, out of print).